GLAMOUR

glamour

15 timeless designs to knit and keep forever

ERIKA KNIGHT
COLLECTABLES

photography by Katya de Grunwald

Quadrille

Editorial director Jane O'Shea
Creative director Helen Lewis
Designer Claire Peters
Project editor Lisa Pendreigh
Editorial assistant Andrew Bayliss
Pattern checker Eva Yates and Sally Harding
Photographer Katya de Grunwald
Photographer's assistant Amy Gwatkin
Stylist Beth Dadswell
Hair and make-up artist Anita Keeling
Model Laure Brosson at Select Model Management
Production director Vincent Smith
Production controller Bridget Fish

First published in 2006 by
Quadrille Publishing Limited
Alhambra House
27–31 Charing Cross Road
London WC2H 0LS
www.quadrille.co.uk

Text and project designs
  © 2006 Erika Knight
Photography
  © 2006 Katya de Grunwald
Design and layout
  © 2006 Quadrille Publishing Limited

British Library Cataloguing-in-Publication
Data: a catalogue record for this book is
available from the British Library.

ISBN-13 978 184400 328 0
ISBN-10 184400 328 0

Printed and bound in China

introduction

Glamour is a must-have portfolio of sensuous knits inspired by Hollywood sirens. Knitwear has never looked so sexy; these garments all provide an easy glamour for both day and evening wear by combining slinky shapes with sumptuous textures. Knit a chevron sweater in mercerized cotton to team with either a clingy pencil skirt or battered denims, or indulge yourself in a lacy knit shrug tied with a shiny ribbon to slip over a delicate camisole. Yarns are sensuous, tactile and opulent: velvet chenille, flowing satin and sensuous silk. The collection is worked in a seductive palette of palest pink, ripe peach and delicate pastel green through to rich teal, gold, damson and grape, and occasionally trimmed with lace and ribbon, or embroidered and beaded.

the glamour collection

the
patterns

sequin scarf

materials

Any fine-weight metallic yarn or fine-weight 4ply mercerized cotton
  yarn, such as Rowan *Lurex Shimmer* or Yeoman's *Cotton Cannele 4ply*
  2 x 25g balls
Pair of 3.25mm knitting needles
Lace, sequins and satin ribbon, each approximately 1.6–1.8m long

size

One size, approximately 140cm long by 8cm wide

tension

29 sts and 41 rows to 10cm over st st using 3.25mm needles

sequin scarf

pattern notes

• Both ends of the scarf have the same broken ladders.
• The dropped sts form the ladders. Make sure they drop to the bottom of the ladder, which is the 'make 1' st. The centre ladder runs the length of the scarf, and the others are random.
• The ladders tend to close up after the stitch is dropped, so pull them apart if they seem to have disappeared.

To make scarf
Using 3.25mm needles, cast on 2 sts.
Row 1 (RS): K to last st, k into front and back of last st.
Row 2: K into front and back of first st, p to last st, k1.
4 sts.
Rep last 2 rows twice more.
8 sts.
Next row (RS): K4, m1, k to last st, k into front and back of last st.
10 sts.
Work in st st **and at the same time** k first and last st of all rows throughout, and cont as foll:
Work 3 rows, inc 1 st on every row as set (1 st at end of every k row and at beg of every p row).
13 sts.
Next row (RS): K9, m1, k to last st, k into front and back of last st.
15 sts.
Work 3 rows, inc 1 st on every row as set.
18 sts.
Next row (RS): K14, m1, k to end.
19 sts.
Note: Shaping at this end of scarf is now complete and 'm1' sts that start ladders have been made.
Work 19 rows straight.
Next row (RS): K4, drop next st, k9, drop next st, k to end.
17 sts.
Work 9 rows straight.
Next row: K4, m1, k9, m1, k to end.
19 sts.
Work 23 rows straight.
Next row (RS): K4, drop next st, k9, drop next st, k to end.
17 sts.
Work 9 rows straight.
Next row (RS): K4, m1, k9, m1, k to end.
19 sts.
Work 23 rows straight.
Next row (RS): K4, drop next st, k9, drop next st, k to end.
17 sts.
Cont on these 17 sts until scarf measures approximately 113cm from cast-on edge, ending with RS

facing for next row.
Next row (RS): K4, m1, k9, m1, k to end.
19 sts.
Work 23 rows straight.
Next row (RS): K4, drop next st, k9, drop next st, k to end.
17 sts.
Work 9 rows straight.
Next row (RS): K4, m1, k9, m1, k to end.
19 sts.
Work 23 rows straight.
Next row (RS): K4, drop next st, k9, drop next st, k to end.
17 sts.
Work 9 rows straight.
Next row (RS): K4, m1, k9, m1,

k to end.
19 sts.
Work 19 rows straight.
Shape end
Next row (RS): K2tog, k2, drop next st, k to end.
17 sts.
Work 3 rows, dec 1 st at end of every p row and at beg of every k row by working k2tog.
14 sts.
Next row (RS): K2tog, k2, drop next st, k to end.
12 sts.
Work 3 rows, dec 1 st on every row as set (1 st at end of every p row and at beg of every k row).
9 sts.

Next row (RS): K2tog, k2, drop next st, k to end.
7 sts.
Cont dec as set until 2 sts rem.
Next row: K2tog.
Fasten off.

To finish
Thread a length of trim through a long ladder, fasten securely and allow some extra length to create a fringe. Thread shorter ladders in same way. Alternatively, leave ladders and trim wide spaces between ladder sts.

ribbed shrug

materials

Any medium-weight wool yarn, such as Rowan *Soft Baby*

    7 (7: 8) x 50g balls

Pair each of 7mm and 8mm knitting needles

7mm circular knitting needle

sizes

dress size	8–10	12–14	16–18	
to fit bust	81–86	91–97	102–107	cm
actual length	45	47	49	cm
cuff to cuff	152	157	162	cm

tension

12 sts and 16 rows to 10cm over st st using 8mm needles and yarn double

To make shrug

Shrug is worked in one piece from cuff to cuff.

Using 7mm needles and two strands of yarn tog, cast on 32 (36: 40) sts.

Rib row 1: *K1, p1, rep from * to end.

Rep last row until shrug measures 15cm from cast-on edge.

Size 8–10 only

Next row: *K1, p into front and back of next st, rep from * to end.

Sizes 12–14 and 16–18 only

Next row: K1, p1, *k1, p into front and back of next st, rep from * to last 2 sts, k1, p1.

48 (52: 58) sts.

Change to 8mm needles and work in rib patt as foll:

Row 1 (RS): *K3, p2, rep from * to last 3 sts, k3.

Row 2: *P3, k2, rep from * to last 3 sts, p3.

Rep these 2 rows until shrug measures 137 (142: 147)cm from cast-on edge, ending with RS facing for next row.

Change to 7mm needles.

Size 8–10 only

Next row (RS): *K1, k2tog, rep from * to end.

Sizes 12–14 and 16–18 only

Next row (RS): K2, *k1, k2tog, rep from * to last 2 sts, k2.

32 (36: 38) sts.

Work 15cm in k1, p1 rib.

Cast off in rib.

To finish

Place markers at both sides of work 53cm in from each cuff.

Fold work in half lengthways and sew cuff and sleeve seam to markers, leaving centre 46 (51: 56)cm unsewn.

Using 7mm circular needle and two strands of yarn tog and with RS facing, pick up and k 150 (162: 180) sts evenly around opening.

Working in rounds, work 12cm in k1, p1 rib.

Cast off in rib.

Weave in any loose yarn ends.

47

lacy tea top

materials

Any fine-weight mohair yarn, such as Rowan *Kidsilk Haze*
    3 (3: 4: 4: 5: 5) x 25g balls
Pair each of 3mm and 3.25mm knitting needles
3.25mm circular knitting needle
6 small buttons, approximately 12mm in diameter
Scrap of organza fabric, approximately 20cm by 4cm
1.8m of matching satin ribbon, 2.5cm wide, for tie

sizes

dress size	8	10	12	14	16	18	
to fit bust	81	86	91	97	102	107	cm
actual bust	81	86	91	97	102	107	cm
length	51	53	53	56	56	59	cm
sleeve seam	6	7	7	7	9	9	cm

tension

25 sts and 32 rows to 10cm over lace patt using 3.25mm needles

49

lacy tea top

stitches
lace pattern

Row 1 and all odd-numbered rows (WS): P.

Rows 2, 4 and 6 (RS): K1, *yon, skp, k1, k2tog, yon, k1, rep from * to end.

Row 8: K2, *yon, sk2p, yon, k3, rep from * ending last rep with k2 instead of k3.

Row 10: K1, *k2tog, yon, k1, yon, skp, k1, rep from * to end.

Row 12: K2tog, *yon, k3, yon, sk2p, rep from * to last 5 sts, yon, k3, yon, skp.

Rep rows 1–12 to form patt.

Back
Using 3mm needles, cast on 103 (109: 115: 121: 127: 133) sts.
K 1 row.
Work first 3 rows of lace patt.
Change to 3.25mm needles and cont in lace patt until back measures 33 (34: 34: 36: 36: 37)cm from cast-on edge, ending with RS facing for next row.

Shape armholes
Keeping to patt as set throughout, cast off 5 sts at beg of next 2 rows.
Dec 1 st each end of next 5 rows, then on foll 6 alt rows.
*71 (77: 83: 89: 95: 101) sts.***
Cont straight until armhole measures 12 (13: 13: 14: 14: 15.5)cm, ending with RS facing for next row.

Divide back
Next row (RS): Work 35 (38: 41: 44: 47: 50) sts, then turn, leaving rem sts on a holder.
Work each side separately.
Cont straight until armhole measures 18 (19: 19: 20: 20: 22)cm, ending with RS facing for next row.

Shape shoulders and neck
Cast off 6 (7: 8: 8: 9: 10) sts at beg of next row, 12 (13: 14: 14: 14: 15) sts at beg of next row, 6 (7: 8: 9: 10: 10) sts at beg of next row, and 4 (4: 4: 4: 4: 4) sts at beg of next row.
Cast off rem 7 (7: 7: 9: 10: 11) sts.
With RS facing, rejoin yarn and k2tog, then patt to end.
35 (38: 41: 44: 47: 50) sts.
Compete to match first side, reversing all shaping.

Front
Work as for back to **.
Cont straight until armhole measures 11.5 (12.5: 12.5: 13.5: 13.5: 14.5)cm, ending with RS facing for next row.

Shape neck
Next row (RS): Work 25 (27: 29: 32: 35: 37) sts, then turn, leaving rem sts on a holder.
Work each side separately.
Dec 1 st at neck edge on next 2 rows, then on foll 2 alt rows, then

on every 4th row until 21 (23: 25: 25: 25: 27) sts rem.

Cont straight until armhole matches back to shoulder, ending with RS facing for next row.

Shape shoulder

Cast off 6 (7: 8: 8: 9: 10) sts at beg of next row and 6 (7: 8: 9: 10: 10) sts on foll alt row.

Cast off rem 7 (7: 7: 9: 10: 11) sts.

With RS facing, rejoin yarn and cast off centre 21 (23: 25: 25: 25: 27) sts, then work to end.

25 (27: 29: 32: 35: 37) sts.

Complete to match first side, reversing all shaping.

Sleeves (make 2)

Using 3mm needles, cast on 72 (77: 77: 77: 82: 87) sts.

Row 1 (RS): P2, * k3, p2, rep from * to end.

Row 2: K2, * p3, k2, rep from * to end.

Rows 3–4: Rep rows 1–2.

Change to 3.25mm needles.

Cont in rib patt as set throughout, inc 1 st each end of next row and every foll 4th row until there are 80 (83: 83: 85: 90: 95) sts, taking increased sts into rib.

Cont straight until sleeve measures 6 (7: 7: 7: 9: 9)cm from cast-on edge, ending with RS facing for next row.

Shape top

Cast off 4 sts at beg next 2 rows.

72 (75: 75: 77: 82: 87) sts.

Dec 1 st each end of next 5 rows.

62 (65: 65: 67: 72: 77) sts.

Dec 1 st each end of foll 3 alt rows, then every foll 4th row until 44 (47: 47: 47: 49: 52: 55) sts rem.

Work 1 row straight.

Dec 1 st each end of next and foll 2 alt rows, then foll 3 rows.

32 (35: 35: 37: 40: 43) sts.

Cast off 4 sts at beg of next 2 rows.

Cast off rem 24 (27: 27: 29: 32: 35) sts.

Frill

Using 3mm needles, cast on 13 sts.

Row 1 (WS): K.

Row 2: P5, turn, k5, turn, p5, k3, p5.

Row 3: K5, turn, p5, turn, p5, k3, p5.

Row 4: K5, turn, p5, turn, k13.

Row 5: P5, turn, k5, turn, k13.

Rep rows 2–5 until frill measures 18cm from cast-on edge, ending with a WS row.

Cast off.

To finish

Weave in any loose yarn ends.

Press pieces gently using a warm iron over a damp cloth.

Sew both shoulder seams.

Picot edgings

Using 3mm circular needle and with RS facing, pick up and k 16 (17: 18: 18: 18: 19) sts along left back neck, 24 sts down left front neck, 21 (23: 25: 25: 25: 27) sts across centre front neck, 24 sts up right front neck, 16 (17: 18: 18: 18: 19) sts along right back neck, 24 sts down right side of back slit, and 24 sts up left side of back slit.

149 (153: 157: 157: 157: 161) sts.

Do not turn but work picot edging around neck edge as foll:

Round 1 (RS): Cast off next 3 sts, *sl st on right-hand needle back onto left-hand needle and use to cast on 2 sts using knit cast-on, cast off 5 sts, rep from * to end. Fasten off.

Sew in sleeves.

Sew side and sleeve seams.

Using 3mm circular needle and with RS facing, pick up and k 206 (218: 230: 242: 254: 266) sts around lower edge of garment, then work picot edging as for neck edge.

Sew one button to centre back neck edge to fasten through lace patt.

Sew frill to centre front, gathering it slightly as it is sewn on.

Cut a strip of organza 4cm wide by 16.5cm long, and sew it to top of knitted frill, gathering it slightly as it is sewn on as before.

Sew on 5 buttons at regular intervals down length of frill.

lace shrug

materials

Any fine-weight 4ply mercerized cotton yarn, such as
Yeoman's *Cotton Cannele 4ply*
1 x 250g cone – or approximately 500 (650: 650)m
Pair of 3.25mm knitting needles
Approximately 2m of satin ribbon, 4cm wide

sizes

dress size	8–10	12–14	16–18	
to fit bust	81–86	91–97	102–107	cm
actual length	40	44	46	cm
width	57	66	74	cm

tension

25 sts and 44 rows to 10cm over lace patt using 3.25mm needles

To make shrug
Shrug is worked in one piece.
Using 3.25mm needles, cast on 145
(163: 181) sts loosely.
**Row 1 and all odd-numbered
rows (WS):** P.
Rows 2, 4 and 6: K1, *yon, skp,
k1, k2tog, yon, k1, rep from * to end.
Row 8: K2, *yon, sk2p, k3, rep
from * ending last rep with k2
instead of k3.
Row 10: K1, *k2tog, yon, k1, yon,
skp, k1, rep from * to end.
Row 12: K2tog, *yon, k3, yon,
sk2p, rep from * to last 5 sts, yon,

k3, yon, skp.
Rep rows 1–12 until shrug measures
38 (42: 44)cm from cast-on edge.
Cast off loosely.

To finish
Weave in any loose yarn ends.
Lay work out flat and gently steam.
Picot edgings
Using 3.25mm needles and with
RS facing, pick up and k 145 (163:
181) sts along cast-on edge of
shrug. Work edging as foll:
Picot row: Cast off 3 sts, *slip st on
right-hand needle back onto left-

hand needle and use to cast on 2 sts
using knit cast-on, cast off 5 sts, rep
from * to end.
Fasten off.
Work picot edging along cast-off
edge in same way.
Work picot edging along each side
edge of shrug in same way, but pick
up 95 (105: 111) sts.
Sew corner seams on edging.
Cut ribbon into four equal pieces,
and sew two pieces each to cast-on
edge and cast-off edge 7.5cm from
side edges.

chevron sweater

materials

Any fine-weight 4-ply mercerized cotton yarn, such as
  Yeoman's *Cotton Cannele 4ply*
  A: 1 x 250g cone in beige – or 680 (680: 680: 850: 850: 850)m
  B: 1 x 250g cone in grey-brown – or 170 (340: 340: 340: 510: 510)m
  C: 1 x 250g cone in blue – or 340 (510: 510: 510: 510: 510)m
  D: 1 x 250g cone in pink – or 510 (510: 680: 680: 680: 680)m
Any fine-weight metallic yarn, such as Rowan *Lurex Shimmer*
  E: 1 x 25g ball in bronze
  F: 1 x 25g ball in red
Pair of 3.25mm knitting needles
Approximately 1.5m of ribbon, 3.5cm wide (optional)

sizes

dress size	8	10	12	14	16	18	
to fit bust	81	86	91	97	102	107	cm
actual bust	84	92	100	108	116	124	cm
length	60	61	63	65	67	68.5	cm
sleeve length	45	47	48	49.5	49.5	51	cm

(from centre back)

tension

41 sts (3 repeats plus 2 sts) to 13cm over chevron patt using
  3.25mm needles

chevron sweater

stitches

chevron pattern

(worked over multiples of 13 sts plus 2 sts)

Row 1 (RS): *K2, m1, k4, sl 1 knitwise, k2tog, psso, k4, m1,
   rep from * to last 2 sts, k2.

Row 2: P.

Rep these 2 rows to form patt, using colours as instructed on
   next page.

Back

Using 3.25mm needles and A, cast on 132 (145: 158: 171: 184: 197) sts.
**Work in chevron patt until back measures 15cm from cast-on edge, ending with RS facing for next row. Cont in chevron patt throughout, working stripes as foll:
Change to E and work 1 row.
Change to B and work 4cm, ending with RS facing for next row.
Change to C and work 9cm, ending with RS facing for next row.
Change to F and work 1 row.**
Change to D and work until back measures 33 (34.5: 35.5: 37: 38: 39)cm from cast-on edge.
Cast off.

Front

Work exactly as for back.

Sleeves (make 2)

Using 3.25mm needles and A, cast on 171 (171: 184: 184: 197: 197) sts.
Work as for back from ** to **.
Change to D and work until sleeve measures 45 (47: 48: 49.5: 49.5: 51)cm from cast-on edge.
Cast off firmly.

To finish

Weave in any loose yarn ends.
Lay pieces out flat and gently steam.
Pin front and back pieces together and sew side seams.
Fold each sleeve in half and pin side edge of sleeve to cast-off edge of body as a yoke, so sleeves meet at centre front and centre back to create V-necklines.
Sew yoke and sleeve seams.
Then sew centre front and back V-seams for about 7.5cm from body to create neck plunge desired.
Cut ribbon in half and sew one piece to each side of back yoke to tie into a bow in centre back or front as desired.

long gloves

materials

Any fine-weight mohair yarn, such as Rowan *Kidsilk Haze*
    2 x 25g balls
Pair each of 2.75mm and 3mm knitting needles

size

One size, to fit woman's medium hand size

tension

32 sts and 40 rows to 10cm over st st using 2.75mm needles

long gloves

pattern notes
• Use mattress stitch to sew glove finger seams for a neat finish.

Right glove
Using 3mm needles, cast on 62 sts very loosely.
Beg with a k row, work in st st, dec 1 st at each end of 3rd row and every foll 8th row until 54 sts rem. Change to 2.75mm needles and cont straight until piece measures 20cm from cast-on edge, ending with RS facing for next row.**
Shape thumb
Row 1 (RS): K28, k into front and back of next st, k2, k into front and back of next st, k22.
56 sts.
Cont in st st throughout, work 3 rows.
Row 5 (RS): K28, k into front and back of next st, k4, k into front and back of next st, k22.
58 sts.
Work 3 rows.
Cont to inc in same way, inc 2 sts on next row and every foll 4th row until there are 68 sts.
Work 3 rows.

Next row (RS): K46, turn, cast on 2 sts.
Next row: P20, turn, cast on 2 sts.
***Work 5cm on these 22 sts, ending with RS facing for next row.
Next row (RS): *K2tog, k2, rep from * to last 2 sts, k2.
Work 1 row.
Next row (RS): *K2tog, rep from * to last st, k1.
9 sts.
Break off yarn and thread end through these 9 sts. Pull up tightly, secure firmly and sew thumb seam.
With RS facing, rejoin yarn and pick up and k 6 sts from base of thumb, then k to end.
56 sts.
Cont straight until piece measures 4cm from pick-up row, ending with RS facing for next row.
Shape first finger
Next row (RS): K36, turn, cast on 1 st.
Next row: P17, turn, cast on 1 st.
18 sts.

Work 6cm on these 18 sts, ending with RS facing for next row.
Next row (RS): *K2tog, k2, * rep from * to last two sts, k2.
Work 1 row.
Next row (RS): *K2tog, rep from * to end.
7 sts.
Break off yarn and thread end through these 7 sts. Pull up tightly, secure firmly and sew finger seam.
Shape second finger
With RS facing, rejoin yarn and pick up and k 2 sts from base of first finger, then k7, turn, cast on 1 st.
Next row (WS): P17, turn, cast on 1 st.
18 sts.
Work 7cm on these 18 sts, ending with RS facing for next row.
Next row (RS): [K2tog, k2] 4 times, k2.
Work 1 row.
Next row (RS): [K2tog] 7 times.
7 sts.

Break off yarn and thread end through these 7 sts. Pull up tightly, secure firmly and sew finger seam.

Shape third finger

With RS facing, rejoin yarn and pick up and k 2 sts from base of second finger, then k7, turn, cast on 1 st.

Next row (WS): P17, turn, cast on 1 st.

18 sts.

Work 6cm on these 18 sts, ending with RS facing for next row.

Next row (RS): [K2tog, k2] 4 times, k2.

Work 1 row.

Next row (RS): [K2tog] 7 times.

7 sts.

Break off yarn and thread end through these 7 sts. Pull up tightly, secure firmly and sew finger seam.

Shape fourth finger

With RS facing, rejoin yarn and pick up and k 4 sts from base of third finger, then k to end.

Next row (WS): P16.

Work 5cm on these 16 sts, ending with RS facing for next row.

Next row (RS): [K2tog, k2] 4 times.

12 sts.

Work 1 row.

Next row (RS): [K2tog] 6 times.

Break off yarn and thread end through these 6 sts. Pull up tightly, secure firmly and sew finger seam and side seam, leaving last 7cm open.

Left glove

Work as for right glove to **.

Shape thumb

Row 1 (RS): K22, k into front and back of next st, k2, k into front and back of next st, k28.

56 sts.

Cont in st st throughout, work 3 rows.

Row 5 (RS): K22, k into front and back of next st, k4, k into front and back of next st, k28.

58 sts.

Work 3 rows.

Cont to inc in same way, inc 2 sts on next row and every foll 4th row until there are 68 sts.

Work 3 rows.

Next row (RS): K40, turn, cast on 2 sts.

Next row: P20, turn, cast on 2 sts.

22 sts.

Complete as for right glove from ***.

Ties (make 2)

Using 3mm needles, cast on 18 sts and work 50cm in st st.

Cast off.

To finish

Weave in any loose yarn ends. Fold each tie in half lengthways to find centre, then pin centre of one tie to centre of cast-on edge of each glove. Sew tie to glove along cast-on edge, leaving excess unattached.

Sew side seams and knot tie ends together.

satin bra top

materials

Any 4ply silk yarn, such as Jaeger *Silk 4ply*
   2 (3: 3) x 50g/1¾oz balls
Pair each of 3.25mm and 4mm knitting needles
Approximately 2m of satin ribbon, 2.5cm wide, for shoulder straps

sizes

dress size	8–10	12–14	16–18	
to fit bust	81–86	91–97	102–107	cm
actual bra-cup				
length	14.5	16	17.5	cm
length from tie end to tie end	96.5	112	127	cm

tension

21 sts and 26 rows to 10cm over st st using 4mm needles and
   yarn double

satin bra top

pattern notes
• Use two strands of the yarn together throughout.

Right front
Using 3.25mm needles and two strands of yarn tog, cast on 38 (44: 50) sts.
Work 4 rows in k1, p1 rib, dec 1 st in centre of last row.
37 (43: 49) sts.
Change to 4mm needles and beg with a k row, work 4 (6: 6) rows in st st.
Next row (RS): K18 (21: 24), m1, k1, m1, k18 (21: 24).
39 (45: 51) sts.
Working in st st throughout, cont to inc 1 st on each side of centre st as set on every foll 4th row until there are 43 (49: 55) sts.
Cont straight for 5 (5: 7) rows, ending with RS facing for next row.

Shape top
Shape top by working short rows as foll:
Next row (RS): K39 (45: 51), bring yarn to front of work between needles, slip next st onto right needle, take yarn to back of work between needles, then slip the slipped st back onto left needle and turn work.
Next row: P35 (41: 47), slip next st onto right needle, take yarn to back of work between needles, then slip the slipped st back onto left needle and turn work.
Cont working 4 sts less on every row as set 8 times more, then turn after last row and k to end.
Next row: P across all sts.
Leave sts on a holder.

Left front
Work exactly as for right front.

Front neck edge
Sew centre front seam, using backstitch and stitching tightly to ease in knitting and slightly shorten seam length.
Using 3.25mm needles and two strands of yarn tog and with RS facing, work in k1, p1 rib across 86 (98: 110) sts from holders.
Work 3 rows more in k1, p1 rib.
Cast off in rib.

Left back
Using 4mm needles and two strands of yarn tog, cast on 26 (29: 31) sts.

Row 1 (RS): K1, p1, k to last st, p1.
Row 2: K1, p to last 2 sts, k1, p1.
Rep rows 1 and 2 once more.
Next row (RS): K1, p1, k to last 3 sts, k2tog, p1.
Cont is st st keeping edge sts as set, work 2 rows.
Next row (WS): K1, p2tog, p to last 2 sts, k1, p1.
Cont as set, dec 1 st at same edge on every 3rd row until 4 sts rem. Dec 1 st at same edge on every foll 4th row twice.
2 sts.
Next row: K2tog.
Fasten off.

Right back
Using 4mm needles and two strands of yarn tog, cast on 26 (29: 31) sts.
Row 1 (RS): P1, k to last 2 sts, p1, k1.
Row 2: P1, k1, p to last st, k1.
Rep rows 1 and 2 once more.
Next row (RS): P1, k2tog, k to last 2 sts, p1, k1.
Cont in st st keeping edge sts as set, work 2 rows.
Next row (WS): P1, k1, p to last 3 sts, p2tog, k1.
Cont as set, dec 1 st at same edge on every 3rd row until 4 sts rem. Dec 1 st at same edge on every foll 4th row twice.
2 sts.
Next row: K2tog.
Fasten off.

To finish
Weave in any loose yarn ends.
Press pieces gently using a warm iron over a damp cloth.
Sew cast-on edges of backs to side seams of fronts, easing in backs to fit.
Cut ribbon into four equal pieces for shoulder straps. Sew one piece to highest point on each bra cup. Tie on bra and mark corresponding positions on bcks for two remaining straps. Sew these straps in place, then tie ribbon straps into bows at shoulder.

chequered cloche

materials

Any fine-weight metallic yarn, such as Rowan *Lurex Shimmer*
   A: 1 x 25g ball in pink
Any fine fine-weight mohair yarn, such as Rowan *Kidsilk Night*
   B: 1 x 25g ball in black
Pair each of 3mm and 3.75mm knitting needles

size

One size

tension

23 sts and 32 rows to 10cm over st st using 3.75mm needles and
   yarn double

chequered cloche

pattern notes

• Use two strands of B held together throughout.
• Use mattress stitch to sew up hat for a neat finish.

To make hat

Using 3mm needles and two strands of yarn tog, cast on 120 sts.
Change to A and work 1 row in k1, p1 rib.
Change to B and work 2 rows in rib as set.
Change to A and work 1 row in rib as set.
Change to 3.75mm needles and k 1 row (WS).
Cont in patt as foll:
Row 1 (RS): Using A, k1, *sl 1 purlwise, k2, rep from * to last 2 sts, sl 1 purlwise, k1.
Row 2: Using A, p.
Row 3: Using B, *sl 1 purlwise, k2, rep from * to end.
Row 4: Using B, p.
Rep last 4 rows until hat measures 12cm from cast-on edge, ending

with WS facing for next row.
Shape crown
Keeping patt correct throughout, shape crown as foll:
Row 1 (WS): [P17, p3tog] 6 times. *108 sts.*
Work 3 rows.
Row 5: [P15, p3tog] 6 times. *96 sts.*
Work 3 rows.
Row 9: [P13, p3tog] 6 times. *84 sts.*
Work 1 row.
Row 11: [P11, p3tog] 6 times. *72 sts.*
Work 1 row.
Row 13: [P9, p3tog] 6 times. *60 sts.*
Work 1 row.
Row 15: [P7, p3tog] 6 times. *48 sts.*

Work 1 row.
Row 17: [P5, p3tog] 6 times. *36 sts.*
Work 1 row.
Row 19: [P3, p3tog] 6 times. *24 sts.*
Work 1 row.
Row 21: [P1, p3tog] 6 times. *12 sts.*
Break off yarn, leaving a long end. Thread end through sts, pull up tightly and fasten off.

To finish
Weave in any loose yarn ends, leaving long end for seam.
Press gently using a warm iron over a damp cloth.
Sew back seam.
Trim with your favourite brooch.

cable sweater

materials

Any super-chunky-weight wool yarn, such as Rowan *Big Wool*
  8 (8: 9: 10: 11: 11) x 100g balls
Pair each of 8mm and 12mm knitting needles
Cable needle
Approximately 5m of sequin trimming (optional)

sizes

dress size	8	10	12	14	16	18	
to fit bust	81	86	91	97	102	107	cm
actual bust	86.5	91.5	101.5	106.5	112	122	cm
length	43	46	48	51	53.5	56	cm
sleeve seam	43	44.5	44.5	46	46	47	cm

tension

8 sts and 12 rows to 10cm over st st using 12mm needles

stitches

C2F (cable 2 front)
Slip next st onto cn and leave at front of work, k1, k1 from cn.
C6F (cable 6 front)
Slip next 3 sts onto cn and leave at front of work, k3, k3 from cn.
moss stitch
(worked over a multiple of 2 sts plus 1 st)
Row 1: K1, *p1, k1, rep from * to end.
  Rep this row.

cable sweater

pattern notes

- Remember to adjust moss stitch when increasing.
- It is easier to attach lengths of sequins with a simple oversew stitch, catching behind the sequins to secure rather than sewing through the holes.

Back

Using 8mm needles, cast on 48 (52: 56: 60: 64: 68) sts.

Work 3 rows k1, p1 rib.

Change to 12mm needles and work as foll:

Sizes 8, 10, 12 and 14 only

Row 1 (RS): Moss st 3 (5: 7: 9: –: –), [p2, k2, p2, k6] 3 times, p2, k2, p2, moss st 3 (5: 7: 9: –: –).

Row 2: Moss st 3 (5: 7: 9: –: –), [k2, p2, k2, p6] 3 times, k2, p2, k2, moss st 3 (5: 7: 9: –: –).

Row 3: Moss st 3 (5: 7: 9: –: –), [p2, C2F, p2, k6] 3 times, p2, C2F, p2, moss st 3 (5: 7: 9: –: –).

Row 4: Rep row 2.

Row 5: Moss st 3 (5: 7: 9: –: –), [p2, C2F, p2, C6F] 3 times, p2, C2F, p2, moss st 3 (5: 7: 9: –: –).

Sizes 16 and 18 only

Row 1 (RS): Moss st – (–: –: –: 7: 9), [p2, k2] twice, [p2, k6, p2, k2] 3 times, p2, k2, p2, moss st – (–: –: –: 7: 9).

Row 2: Moss st – (–: –: –: 7: 9), [k2, p2] twice, [k2, p6, k2, p2] 3 times, k2, p2, k2, moss st – (–: –: –: 7: 9).

Row 3: Moss st – (–: –: –: 7: 9), [p2, C2F] twice, [p2, k6, p2, C2F] 3 times, p2, C2F, p2, moss st – (–: –: –: 7: 9).

Row 4: Rep row 2.

Row 5: Moss st – (–: –: –: 7: 9), [p2, C2F] twice, [p2, C6F, p2, C2F] 3 times, p2, C2F, p2, moss st – (–: –: –: 7: 9).

All sizes

Row 6: Rep row 2.

Row 7: Rep row 3.

Row 8: Rep row 2.

Rep rows 3–8 until back measures 29 (31: 33: 35: 37: 39)cm from cast-on edge, ending with RS facing for next row.

Shape armholes

Keeping patt correct as set throughout, cast off 2 sts at beg of next 2 rows.

Dec 1 st at each end of next 4 (4: 4: 6: 6: 6) rows.

36 (40: 44: 44: 48: 52) sts.

Work 10 (12: 14: 14: 16: 16) rows straight.

Cast off loosely.

Front

Work exactly as for back.

Sleeves (make 2)

Using 8mm needles, cast on 24 (24: 27: 27: 30: 30) sts.

Row 1 (RS): *K2, p1, rep from * to end.

Row 2: *K1, p2, rep from * to end.

Rep rows 1 and 2 until sleeve measures 8cm from cast-on edge, ending with WS facing for next row.

Next row (WS): Rib as set, inc at end of row on sizes 12 and 14 and each end of row on sizes 16 and 18. *24 (24: 28: 28: 32: 32) sts.*

Change to 12mm needles.

Work in patt as foll **and at the**

same time inc 1 st at each end of 5th and every foll 14th (14th: 14th: 14th: 14th: 16th) row until there are 30 (30: 34: 34: 38: 38) sts, taking inc sts into moss st.

Row 1 (RS): Moss st 3 (3: 5: 5: 7: 7), p2, k2, p2, k6, p2, k2, p2, moss st 3 (3: 5: 5: 7: 7).

Row 2: Moss st 3 (3: 5: 5: 7: 7), k2, p2, k2, p6, k2, p2, k2, moss st 3 (3: 5: 5: 7: 7).

Row 3: Moss st 3 (3: 5: 5: 7: 7), p2, C2F, p2, k6, p2, C2F, p2, moss st 3 (3: 5: 5: 7: 7).

Row 4: Rep row 2.

Row 5: Work as for row 3 but inc at each end and working C6F instead of k6.

Row 6: Work as for row 2 but with 1 extra moss st at each end.

Row 7: Work as for row 3 but with 1 extra moss st at each end.

Row 8: Work as for row 2 but with 1 extra moss st at each end.

Rep rows 3–8 until sleeve measures 43 (44.5: 44.5: 46: 46: 47)cm from cast-on edge, ending with RS facing for next row.

Shape top
Keeping patt correct as set throughout, cast off 2 sts at beg of next 2 rows.
26 (26: 30: 30: 34: 34) sts.
Dec 1 st at each end of next and every foll alt row until 8 (10: 12: 10: 12: 11) sts rem.
Work 1 row.
Cast off.

To finish
Weave in any loose yarn ends.
Lay work out flat and gently steam.
Sew sleeves into armholes, leaving left back armhole seam open.

Neckband
Using 8mm needles and with RS facing, pick up and k 8 (10: 12: 10: 12: 12) sts across top of sleeve, 36 (40: 44: 44: 48: 52) sts across front, 8 (10: 12: 10: 12: 12) sts across top of sleeve, and 36 (40: 44: 44: 48: 52) sts across back.
88 (100: 112: 108: 120: 128) sts.

Row 1: *P2, k1, rep from * to last 1 (1: 1: 0: 0: 2) sts, p1 (1: 1: 0: 0: 2).

Row 2: K1 (1: 1: 0: 0: 2), *p1, k2, rep from * to end.

Rep last 2 rows until rib measures 6 (6: 6: 8: 8: 8)cm.
Cast off loosely.

Sew left back armhole seam. Sew side and sleeve seams. Cut sequin trimming into 65cm lengths and stitch to cable weaving under and over as you attach, following curve of cable.

beaded jewellery

materials

For button bracelet

Any fine-weight 4ply cotton yarn or fine-weight mohair yarn,
such as Yeoman's *Cotton Cannele 4ply* and Rowan *Kidsilk Haze*
1 x 25g ball

1 spool of fine silver beading wire

Pair of 3mm knitting needles

Button for fastening

Assorted buttons, beads and sequins for decoration

Matching thread for sewing on decoration

For buckle bracelet

Any fine-weight 4ply cotton yarn or fine-weight mohair yarn,
such as Yeoman's *Cotton Cannele 4ply* and Rowan *Kidsilk Haze*
2 x 25g balls

1 spool of fine silver beading wire

Pair of 3mm knitting needles

Buckle for fastening

Assorted buttons, beads and sequins for decoration

Matching thread for sewing on decoration

For choker

Any fine-weight 4ply cotton yarn or fine-weight mohair yarn,
such as Yeoman's *Cotton Cannele 4ply* and Rowan *Kidsilk Haze*
1 x 25g or ball

1 spool of fine silver beading wire

Pair of 3mm knitting needles

Approximately 1m of satin ribbon, 1.5cm wide, for ties

Assorted buttons, beads and sequins for decoration

Matching thread for sewing on decoration

beaded jewellery

sizes

Button bracelet: approximately 22cm long by 3cm wide
Buckle bracelet: approximately 24cm long by 3cm wide
Choker: approximately 30cm long by 3cm wide

tension

29 sts and 39 rows to 10cm over st st using 3mm needles.

pattern notes

• Use one strand of yarn with one strand of fine wire together
  throughout.
• For decoration, collect old buttons and beads of various sizes and
  shapes in your desired colour scheme.

To make button bracelet

Using 3mm needles and one strand of yarn and one strand of wire held tog, cast on 10 sts.

Beg with a k row, work 4 rows in st st.

Make buttonhole as foll:

Next row (RS): K4, cast off next 2 sts, k to end.

Next row: P4, cast on 2 sts, p to end.

Work 6 rows st st, then rep buttonhole rows.

Cont in st st until bracelet measures 22cm (or desired length) from cast-on edge.

Cast off.

To finish

Weave in any loose yarn ends. Wrap band around wrist, mark where button should fasten and sew on button.

To embellish

Sew on buttons, beads and sequins randomly, clustering them together for maximum impact.

To make buckle bracelet

Using 3mm needles and one strand of yarn and one strand of wire held tog, cast on 4 sts.

Beg with a k row, work 4 rows st st. Cont in st st throughout, inc 1 st at each end of next row and every foll 6th row twice. *10 sts.*

Work 17cm on these 10 sts, ending with RS facing for next row.

Shape end of buckle as foll:

Dec 1 st at each end of next and foll 4th row. *6 sts.*

P 1 row.

Cast off.

To finish

Weave in any loose yarn ends. Thread cast-on edge through buckle bar and sew in place to secure buckle.

To embellish

Sew on buttons, beads and sequins randomly, clustering them together for maximum impact.

To make choker

Using 3mm needles and one strand of yarn and one strand of wire held tog, cast on 8 sts.

Beg with a k row, work in st st until choker measures 30cm from cast-on edge.

Cast off.

To finish

Weave in any loose yarn ends. Cut ribbon in half and sew one piece to each end of choker for ties.

To embellish

Sew on buttons, beads and sequins randomly, clustering them together for maximum impact.

vintage handbag

materials

Any chunky-weight ribbon/tape yarn, such as Louisa Harding
   Sari Ribbon or Colinette *Giotto*
   A: 1 x 50g ball Louisa Harding *Sari Ribbon*
   B: 1 x 100g hank Colinette *Giotto*
Pair of 6mm or 7mm knitting needles
Clasp, approximately 15cm wide for ribbed version and 11cm wide
   for stocking stitch version
Piece of fabric for lining, approximately 40cm by 30cm for one bag,
   and matching sewing thread
Approximately 45cm of satin ribbon, 3.5cm wide, for handle for
   one bag

sizes

Ribbed version: one size, 15cm long by 25cm wide across lower edge
Stocking stitch version: one size, 15.5cm long by 18cm wide
   across lower edge

tension

Ribbed version: 16 sts and 20 rows to 10cm over st st using
   6mm needles and A
Stocking stitch version: 12 sts and 21 rows to 10cm over st st
   using 7mm needles and B

vintage handbag

pattern note

• The handbag in the phto is the ribbed version. The stocking stitch version of the handbag is provided as a quicker alternative.

To make ribbed version of bag
Using 6mm needles and A, cast on
26 sts.
Row 1: *K1, p1, rep from * to end.
Row 2: Sl 1 st knitwise, *p1, k into
next st but through loop of row
below **and at the same time** slip
st above off needle, rep from * to
last st, p1.
Rep row 2 until bag measures 30cm
from cast-on edge.
Cast off in rib.

To finish
Cut lining fabric to same size as
knitted piece, adding 1.5cm all
around for seam allowance.
Fold knitting in half widthways
with RS together and sew side
seams, leaving top end open to
attach to clasp.
Sew lining side seams in same way
and insert lining into bag. Fold
under hem at top of lining and sew
in place to top edge of bag.
Attach cast-on and cast-off edges of
bag to clasp, easing in knitting as
required. Sew ribbon handle to
clasp or bag.

**To make stocking stitch
version of bag**
Using 7mm needles and B, cast on
6 sts.
P 1 row.
Next row (inc row) (RS): K1, k
into front and back of next st, m1,
k to last 3 sts, m1, k into front and
back of next st, k2.
10 sts.
Next row: P.
Rep last 2 rows twice more.
18 sts.
Cont in st st throughout, work 8
rows straight.
Next row: Rep inc row.
22 sts.
Cont straight until bag measures
24cm, from cast-on edge, ending
with RS facing for next row.
Next row (dec row) (RS): K2,
k3tog tbl, k to last 5 sts, k3tog, k2.
18 sts.
Work 9 rows straight.
Next row: Rep dec row.
14 sts.
Next row: P.
Rep last 2 rows twice more.
6 sts.
Cast off.

To finish
Finish as for ribbed version of bag.

cable waistcoat

materials

Any fine-weight metallic yarn, such as Rowan *Lurex Shimmer*
   9 (9: 10: 10: 11) x 25g balls
Pair each of 3mm and 3.25mm knitting needles
3mm circular knitting needle
5 to 7 press studs
5 to 7 mother-of-pearl buttons

sizes

dress size	8	10	12	14	16	18	
to fit bust	81	86	91	97	102	107	cm
actual bust	76	81	86	91	97	102	cm
length	43	43	45	47	48	50	cm

tension

32 sts and 32 rows to 10cm over single rib using 3.25mm needles
36 sts and 32 rows to 10cm over cable patt using 3.25mm needles

stitches

C2F (cable 2 front)
Slip next st onto cn and leave at front of work, k1, k1 from cn.
C6F (cable 6 front)
Slip next 3 sts onto cn and leave at front of work, k3, k3 from cn.

cable waistcoat

Back

Using 3.25mm needles, cast on
110 (118: 126: 134: 142: 150) sts.
Work in k1, p1 rib throughout as foll:

Sizes 8 and 10 only

Inc 1 st at each end of 7th row and
every foll 6th row until there are
136 (144) sts.

Sizes 12, 14, 16 and 18 only

Inc 1 st at each end of 7th row
and every foll 6th and 7th row
alternately until there are
– (–: 152: 160: 168: 176) sts.

All sizes

Cont straight until 86 rows have
been completed and work measures
24 (24: 25.5: 25.5: 25.5: 27)cm from
cast-on edge.

Shape armholes

Cast off 5 (5: 5: 5: 5: 5) sts at beg
of next 2 rows, 4 (4: 4: 5: 5: 5) sts
at beg of foll 2 rows, 3 (3: 4: 4: 4: 4)
sts at beg of foll 2 (2: 2: 2: 2: 4)
rows, and 2 sts at beg of next 4
(6: 6: 6: 6: 6) rows.
104 (108: 114: 120: 128: 128) sts.
Dec 1 st at each end of next row
and every foll alt row until 98 (102:

106: 110: 114: 116) sts rem.
Cont straight until armhole measures
19 (19: 20: 21.5: 23: 24)cm.

Shape shoulders and neck

Cast off 9 (9: 9: 10: 11: 12) sts at
beg of next 2 rows.

Next row: Cast off 9 (9: 10: 10:
11: 11) sts, work until there are
13 (14: 15: 15: 15: 15) sts on right-
hand needle, then turn, leaving rem
sts on a holder.
Work each side separately.
Cast off 4 sts at beg of next row.
Cast off rem 9 (10: 11: 11: 11: 11) sts.
Rejoin yarn to rem stitches on
holder, cast off centre 36 (38: 38:
40: 40: 40) sts and work to end.
Cast off 9 (9: 10: 10: 11: 11) sts at
beg of next row and 4 sts at beg of
foll row.
Cast off rem 9 (10: 11: 11: 11: 11) sts.

Left front

Using 3.25mm needles, cast on 4 sts.

Row 1 (RS): K4, cast on 2 sts. *6 sts.*

Row 2: K1, p5, cast on 3 sts. *9 sts.*

Row 3: P2, k6, p1, cast on 2 sts.
11 sts.

Row 4: P1, k2, p6, k2, cast on
3 sts. *14 sts.*

Row 5: P1, C2F, p2, C6F, p2, k1,
cast on 2 sts. *16 sts.*

Row 6: K1, p2, k2, p6, k2, p2, k1,
cast on 3 sts. *19 sts.*

Row 7: K2, p2, C2F, p2, k6, p2,
C2F, p1, cast on 2 sts. *21 sts.*

Row 8: P1, k2, p2, k2, p6, [k2, p2]
twice, cast on 3 sts. *24 sts.*

Row 9: K5, p2, C2F, p2, k6, p2,
C2F, p2, k1, cast on 2 sts. *26 sts.*

Row 10: P3, k2, p2, k2, p6, k2, p2,
k2, p5, cast on 3 sts. *29 sts.*

Row 11: P2, k6, p2, C2F, p2, C6F,
p2, C2F, p2, k3, cast on 2 sts. *31 sts.*

Row 12: P5, [k2, p2, k2, p6] twice,
k2, cast on 3 sts. *34 sts.*

Row 13: P1, C2F, p2, [k6, p2, C2F,
p2] twice, k5, cast on 2 sts. *36 sts.*

Row 14: K1, p6, [k2, p2, k2, p6]
twice, k2, p2, k1, cast on 3 sts.
39 sts.

Row 15: K2, [p2, C2F, p2, k6]
3 times, p1, cast on 2 sts. *41 sts.*

Row 16: P1, k2, [p6, k2, p2, k2]
3 times, p2, cast on 3 sts. *44 sts.*

Row 17: K5, [p2, C2F, p2, C6F]

3 times, p2, k1, cast on 2 sts. *46 sts.*
Row 18: K1, [p2, k2, p6, k2]
3 times, p2, k2, p5, cast on 3 sts. *49 sts.*
Row 19: [P2, k6, p2, C2F] 4 times,
p1, cast on 2 sts. *51 sts.*
Row 20: K3, [p2, k2, p6, k2]
4 times, cast on 4 (8: 3: 3: 3: 3) sts.
55 (59: 54: 54: 54: 54) sts.
Row 21: P2 (6: 1: 1: 1: 1), [C2F,
p2, k6, p2] 4 times, C2F, p3, cast
on 5 sts (for centre front band).
60 (64: 59: 59: 59: 59) sts.
Row 22: [P1, k1] twice, p1, k3, [p2,
k2, p6, k2] 4 times, p2, k2 (6: 1: 1:
1: 1), cast on 0 (0: 5: 3: 3: 3) sts.
60 (64: 64: 62: 62: 62) sts.

Sizes 8, 10 and 12 only
Row 23 (RS): P2 (6: 6), [C2F, p2,
C6F, p2] 4 times, C2F, p3, [k1, p1]
twice, k1.
Row 24: [P1, k1] twice, p1, k3, [p2,
k2, p6, k2] 4 times, p2, k2 (6: 6),
cast on 0 (0: 4) sts. *60 (64: 68) sts.*
Row 25: P2 (6: 10), [C2F, p2, k6,
p2] 4 times, C2F, p3, [k1, p1]
twice, k1.
Row 26: [P1, k1] twice, p1, k3, [p2,
k2, p6, k2] 4 times, p2, k2 (6: 10).

Sizes 14, 16 and 18 only
Row 23 (RS): K2, [p2, C2F, p2,
C6F] 4 times, p2, C2F, p3, [k1, p1]
twice, k1.
Row 24: [P1, k1] twice, p1, k3,
[p2, k2, p6, k2] 4 times, p2, k2, p2,
cast on 5 sts. – (–: –: 67: 67: 67) sts.
Row 25: P1, k6, [p2, C2F, p2, k6]
4 times, p2, C2F, p3, [k1, p1]
twice, k1.
Row 26: [P1, k1] twice, p1, k3, [p2,
k2, p6, k2] 4 times, p2, k2, p6, k1,

cast on 5 sts. – (–: –: 72: 72: 72) sts.
Row 27: [P2, C2F, p2, k6] 5 times,
p2, C2F, p3, [k1, p1] twice, k1.
Row 28: [P1, k1] twice, p1, k3,
[p2, k2, p6, k2] 5 times, p2, k2,
cast on – (–: –: 0: 4: 8) sts.
– (–: –: 72: 76: 80) sts.
Row 29: P – (–: –: 2: 6: 10),
[C2F, p2, C6F, p2] 5 times, C2F,
p3, [k1, p1] twice, k1.
Row 30: [P1, k1] twice, p1, k3,
[p2, k2, p6, k2] 5 times, p2, k
– (–: –: 2: 6: 10).

All sizes
This sets patt, with 5-st k1, p1 rib at
centre front edge, 5 (5: 5: 6: 6) C2F
cables (crossed on every RS row),
4 (4: 4: 5: 5: 5) C6F cable panels
(crossed on every 6th row), and
2 (6: 10: 2: 6: 10) sts in rev st st at
side-seam edge.
There are *60 (64: 68: 72: 76: 80) sts*
and RS is facing for next row.
Side-seam shaping
**Keeping to patt as set throughout,
work 2 (2: 6: 6: 6: 6) rows in patt,
ending with RS facing for next row.
Inc 1 st at beg (side-seam edge) of
next row, then at same edge on
every foll 6th row 12 times, taking
all inc sts into rev st st, ending with
WS facing for next row.
*73 (77: 81: 85: 89: 93) sts.***
Work 5 rows straight, ending with
RS facing for next row.
**Neck, armhole and shoulder
shaping**
Sizes 8 and 10 only
Next row (RS): Cast off 5 sts (at
armhole edge), patt to last 8 sts,

p2tog, p1, slip rem 5 sts onto a
safety pin. *62 (66) sts.*
Work 1 row straight.
To shape armhole, cast off 4 sts at
beg of next row, 3 sts at beg of foll
alt row, 2 sts at beg of foll 2 alt
rows, then dec 1 st at beg of foll
2 alt rows, **and at the same time**
beg shaping V-neck by dec 1 st at
end (neck edge) of next row and
at neck edge on every foll alt row
5 times, ending with WS facing for
next row. *43 (47) sts.*
Work 1 row straight.
***Keeping armhole edge straight,
dec 1 st at neck edge on next row,
then at same edge on every foll alt
row twice, then on every foll 3rd
row 15 times. *25 (29) sts.*
Work 2 rows straight, ending with
RS facing for next row.***
Next row (RS): Cast off 5 (9) sts,
patt to last 2 sts, work last 2 sts tog.
19 sts.
Work 1 row straight.
Cast off 9 sts at beg of next row.
10 sts.
Dec 1 st at beg of next row.
Cast off rem 9 sts.

Sizes 12, 14, 16 and 18 only
Next row (RS): Patt to last 8 sts,
p2tog, p1, slip rem 5 sts onto a
safety pin. – (–: 75: 79: 83: 87) sts.
Work 1 row straight.
Dec 1 st at end (neck edge) of next
row, then at same edge on every foll
alt row – (–: 0: 0: 1: 2) times.
– (–: 74: 78: 81: 84) sts.
Work 1 row straight.
To shape armhole, cast off 5 sts at

beg of next row, 4 sts at beg of foll alt row, 3 sts at beg of foll alt row, 2 sts at beg of foll 2 alt rows, then dec 1 st at beg of foll 2 alt rows, **and at the same time** cont shaping V-neck by dec 1 st at end (neck edge) of next row and on every foll alt row - (-: 6: 6: 6: 5) times, ending with WS facing for next row.

– (–: 49: 53: 56: 60) sts.

Work – (–: 1: 1: 2: 0) rows straight. Keeping armhole edge straight, dec 1 st at neck edge on next row and every foll 3rd row – (–: 17: 19: 19: 19) times. *– (–: 31: 33: 36: 40) sts.*

Size 12 only

Work 2 rows straight, ending at armhole edge.

Next row (RS): Cast off 9 sts, patt to last 2 sts, work last 2 sts tog. *21 sts.*

Work 1 row straight.

Cast off 10 sts.

Cast off rem 11 sts.

Sizes 14, 16 and 18 only

Work – (–: –: 0: 1: 5) rows straight, ending at armhole edge.

Cast off – (-: -: 11: 12: 13) sts at beg of next row and foll alt row.

Cast off rem – (–: –: 11: 12: 14) sts.

Right front

Using 3.25mm needles, cast on 4 sts.

Row 1 (RS): K4.

Row 2: P4, cast on 2 sts. *6 sts.*

Row 3: P1, k5, cast on 3 sts. *9 sts.*

Row 4: K2, p6, k1, cast on 2 sts. *11 sts.*

Row 5: K1, p2, C6F, p2, cast on 3 sts. *14 sts.*

Row 6: K1, p2, k2, p6, k2, p1, cast on 2 sts. *16 sts.*

Row 7: P1, C2F, p2, k6, p2, C2F, p1, cast on 3 sts. *19 sts.*

Row 8: [P2, k2] twice, p6, k2, p2, k1, cast on 2 sts. *21 sts.*

Row 9: K1, p2, C2F, p2, k6, p2, C2F, p2, k2, cast on 3 sts. *24 sts.*

Row 10: P5, k2, p2, k2, p6, k2, p2, k2, p1, cast on 2 sts. *26 sts.*

Row 11: K3, p2, C2F, p2, C6F, p2, C2F, p2, k5, cast on 3 sts. *29 sts.*

Row 12: [K2, p6, k2, p2] twice, k2, p3, cast on 2 sts. *31 sts.*

Row 13: K5, [p2, C2F, p2, k6] twice, p2, cast on 3 sts. *34 sts.*

Row 14: K1, [p2, k2, p6, k2] twice, p2, k2, p5, cast on 2 sts. *36 sts.*

Row 15: P1, [k6, p2, C2F, p2] twice, k6, p2, C2F, p1, cast on 3 sts. *39 sts.*

Row 16: P2, [k2, p2, k2, p6] 3 times, k1, cast on 2 sts. *41 sts.*

Row 17: K1, [p2, C6F, p2, C2F] 3 times, p2, k2, cast on 3 sts. *44 sts.*

Row 18: P5, [k2, p2, k2, p6] 3 times, k2, p1, cast on 2 sts. *46 sts.*

Row 19: P1, [C2F, p2, k6, p2] 3 times, C2F, p2, k5, cast on 3 sts. *49 sts.*

Row 20: [K2, p6, k2, p2] 4 times, k1, cast on 2 sts. *51 sts.*

Row 21: P3, [C2F, p2, k6, p2] 4 times, cast on 4 (8: 3: 3: 3: 3) sts. *55 (59: 54: 54: 54: 54) sts.*

Row 22: K2 (6: 1: 1: 1: 1), [p2, k2, p6, k2] 4 times, p2, k3, cast on 5 sts (for centre front band). *60 (64: 59: 59: 59: 59) sts.*

Row 23: [K1, p1] twice, k1, p3, [C2F, p2, C6F, p2] 4 times, C2F, p2 (6: 1: 1: 1: 1), cast on 0 (0: 5: 3: 3: 3) sts. *60 (64: 64: 62: 62: 62) sts.*

Sizes 8, 10 and 12 only

Row 24 (WS): K2 (6: 6), [p2, k2, p6, k2] 4 times, p2, k3, [p1, k1] twice, p1.

Row 25: [K1, p1] twice, k1, p3, [C2F, p2, k6, p2] 4 times, C2F, p2 (6: 6), cast on 0 (0: 4) sts. *60 (64: 68) sts.*

Row 26: K2 (6: 10), [p2, k2, p6, k2] 4 times, p2, k3, [p1, k1] twice, p1.

Sizes 14, 16 and 18 only

Row 24 (WS): P2, [k2, p2, k2, p6] 4 times, k2, p2, k3, [p1, k1] twice, p1.

Row 25: [K1, p1] twice, k1, p3, [C2F, p2, k6, p2] 4 times, C2F, p2, k2, cast on 5 sts.

– (–: –: 67: 67: 67) sts.

Row 26: K1, [p6, k2, p2, k2] 4 times, p6, k2, p2, k3, [p1, k1] twice, p1.

Row 27: [K1, p1] twice, k1, p3, [C2F, p2, k6, p2] 4 times, C2F, p2, k6, p1, cast on 5 sts.

– (–: –: 72: 72: 72) sts.

Row 28: [K2, p2, k2, p6] 5 times, k2, p2, k3, [p1, k1] twice, p1.

Row 29: [K1, p1] twice, k1, p3, [C2F, p2, C6F, p2] 5 times, C2F, p2, cast on – (–: –: 0: 4: 8) sts.

– (–: –: 72: 76: 80) sts.

Row 30: K – (–: –: 2: 6: 10), [p2, k2, p6, k2] 5 times, p2, k3, [p1, k1] twice, p1.

All sizes

This sets patt, with 5-st k1, p1 rib at centre front edge, 5 (5: 5: 6: 6) C2F cables (crossed on every RS row), 4 (4: 4: 5: 5: 5) C6F cable panels (crossed on every 6th row), and 2 (6: 10: 2: 6: 10) sts in rev st st at side-seam edge.

There are *60 (64: 68: 72: 76: 80) sts* and RS is facing for next row.

Side-seam shaping

Work as for left front from ** to **.

Work 6 rows straight, ending with WS facing for next row.

Neck, armhole and shoulder shaping

Sizes 8 and 10 only

Next row (WS): Cast off 5 sts (at armhole edge), patt to last 8 sts, k2tog, k1, slip rem 5 sts onto a safety pin. *62 (66) sts.*

To beg V-neck shaping, dec 1 st at beg of next row (neck edge) and at neck edge on every foll alt row 5 times, **and at the same time** shape armhole by casting off 4 sts at beg of foll alt row, 3 sts at beg of foll alt row, 2 sts at beg of foll 2 alt rows, then dec 1 st at armhole edge of foll 2 alt rows, ending with RS facing for next row. *43 (47) sts.*

Work as for left front from *** to ***.

Dec 1 st at beg of next row. *24 (28) sts.*

Cast off 5 (9) sts at beg of next row. *19 sts.*

Work 1 row straight.

Next row (WS): Cast off 9 sts, patt to last 2 sts, work last 2 sts tog. Cast off rem 9 sts.

Sizes 12, 14, 16 and 18 only

Next row (WS): Patt to last 8 sts, k2tog, k1, slip rem 5 sts onto a safety pin. *– (–: 75: 89: 83: 87) sts.*

Dec 1 st at end (neck edge) of next

row, then at same edge on every foll alt row – (–: 1: 1: 2: 3) times.

– (–: 73: 77: 80: 83) sts.

Work 1 row straight.

To shape armhole, cast off 5 sts at beg of next row, 4 sts at beg of foll alt row, 3 sts at beg of foll alt row, 2 sts at beg of foll 2 alt rows, then dec 1 st at beg of foll 2 alt rows,

and at the same time cont shaping V-neck by dec 1 st at beg (neck edge) of every foll alt row – (–: 7: 7: 6: 5) times, and every foll 3rd row – (–: 0: 0: 0: 1) time.

– (–: 48: 52: 56: 59) sts.

Work – (–: 2: 2: 1: 2) rows straight.

Keeping armhole edge straight, dec 1 st at neck edge on next row and every foll 3rd row – (–: 17: 18: 19: 18) times. *– (–: 30: 33: 36: 40) sts.*

Work – (–: 0: 1: 2: 6) rows straight, ending at armhole edge.

Cast off – (–: 9: 11: 12: 13) sts at beg of next row and – (–: 10: 11: 12: 13) sts at beg of foll alt row.

Cast off rem – (–: 11: 11: 12: 14) sts.

To finish

Weave in any loose yarn ends.

Sew both shoulder seams.

Front lapel and collar

Using 3.25mm needles and with RS of work facing, rejoin yarn to one set of 5 sts left on safety pin and working in rib as set, inc 1 st at inside edge on next and every foll alt row until there are 30 sts, ending at straight edge.

Cast off first 16 sts, return st on right-hand needle to left-hand

needle and cast on 16 sts, rib to end.

Cont straight until collar fits without stretching to centre back neck.

Cast off in rib.

Work other side to match, reversing all shaping.

Picot edgings

Using 3mm circular needle and with RS facing, pick up and k 125 (125: 131: 137: 143: 149) sts evenly along edge of armhole.

Work picot edging as foll:

Row 1 (WS): Cast off 3 sts, *slip st on right-hand needle back onto left-hand needle and use to cast on 2 sts using knit cast-on, cast off 5 sts, rep from * to end.

Fasten off.

Sew side seams.

Work picot edging around lower edge as foll:

Using 3mm circular needle with RS facing, pick up and k 4 sts along left front band, 30 sts along left front slope, 40 (44: 50: 54: 60: 64) sts along other side of left front slope, 106 (112: 118: 124: 130: 136) sts across back, 40 (44: 50: 54: 60: 64) sts along right front slope, 30 sts along other right front slope, and 4 sts along right front band.

254 (268: 286: 300: 318: 332) sts.

Work picot edging as for armhole edging.

Fasten off.

Sew press studs evenly spaced along front edge to start of V-neck shaping.

Sew a button on top of each press stud.

jacquard scarf

materials

Any chunky-weight wool yarn, such as Debbie Bliss *Maya*
    A: 1 x 100g hank in pink
Any medium-weight wool yarn, such as Rowan *RYC Soft Lux*
    B: 1 x 50g ball in purple
Any fine-weight mohair yarn, such as Rowan *Kidsilk Haze*
    C: 1 x 25g ball in lilac
    D: 3 x 25g balls in teal
Any chunky-weight wool yarn, such as Debbie Bliss *Maya*
    E: 3 x 100g hanks in a multi-colour
Any chunky-weight ribbon/tape yarn, such as Louisa Harding
    Fauve Tape
    F: 2 x 50g balls in green
Pair each of 6.5mm and 7mm knitting needles
Approximately 50cm of lace (optional)
Beads and sequins (optional)

size

One size, approximately 190cm long by 35cm wide

tension

Each yarn will have a separate tension; this has been calculated
    in the overall size of the scarf.

jacquard scarf

pattern notes

- Use one strand of B together with one strand of C.
- Use three strands of D together.
- Use one strand only of A, E and F.

To make scarf

Using 6.5mm needles and one strand of A, cast on 42 sts.

Rib row 1 (RS): [K1, p1] 3 times, *k2, p1, rep from * to end.

Rib row 2: *K1, p2, rep from * to last 6 sts, [k1, p1] 3 times.

Rep last 2 rows until scarf measures 3cm from the cast-on edge, ending with RS facing for next row.

Change to one strand of B and one strand of C held tog.

Next row (RS): [K1, p1] 3 times, k to end.

Next row: P to last 6 sts, [k1, p1] 3 times.

Rep last 2 rows until BC stripe measures 15cm, ending with RS facing for next row.

Change to three strands of D held tog.

Keeping to st st with 6-st k1, p1 rib along right edge as set throughout, work until D stripe measures 7.5cm, ending with RS facing for next row.

Change to one strand of E.

Work until E stripe measures 145cm, ending with RS facing for next row.

Break off E.

Beg each stripe on a RS row, work D stripe then BC stripe, working same number of rows as before and ending with RS facing for next row.

Change to one strand of A and rep rib rows 1 and 2 until rib measures 3cm.

Cast off in rib.

Edging

Using 7mm needles and one strand of F, cast on 12 sts. Work in k1, p1 rib until edging fits length of scarf. Cast off in rib.

To finish

Weave in any loose yarn ends.

Press pieces gently, using a warm iron over a damp cloth and avoiding ribbing.

Sew edging to side of scarf without ribbing.

Cut two random shapes from lace, cutting around lace motifs.

Lay one cut-out lace shape on each end of scarf and sew in place.

If desired, embellish each end of scarf with randomly placed sequins and beads.

chinoiserie cardigan

materials

Any 4ply-weight cotton yarn, such as Rowan *RYC Cashcotton 4ply*
    8 (8: 9: 10: 10: 11) x 50g balls
Pair each of 3mm and 3.25mm knitting needles
Approximately 1m of lining fabric (optional) and matching
    sewing thread
Fine-weight metallic yarn or embroidery thread, in bronze,
    for embroidery
Pale pink, pale green and bronze sequins
Gold bugle beads
7 to 8 press studs
7 to 8 mother-of-pearl buttons

sizes

dress size	8	10	12	14	16	18	
to fit bust	81	86	91	97	102	107	cm
actual bust	84	90	95	100	105	110	cm
length	49.5	52	54.5	57	57	60	cm
sleeve seam	30.5	32	33	34	35.5	37	cm

tension

25 sts and 36 rows to 10cm over st st using 3.25mm needles

chinoiserie cardigan

pattern notes

- Work increases and decreases three sts inside the edges and knit through the back of loops to create a fully fashioned detail as follows:

  On a k row: k3, k2tog, k to last 5 sts, k2tog tbl, k3.

  On a p row: p3, p3tog tbl, p to last 5 sts, p2tog, p3.

- Work the centre front bands integrally with each front to give a neater finish.

- Increases are made through the sleeve cuffs.

Back

Using 3mm needles, cast on 101 (107: 113: 119: 125: 131) sts.

Rib row 1 (RS): *P1, k1, rep from * to last st, p1.

Row 2: *K1, p1, rep from * to last st, k1.

Rep last 2 rows until ribbing measures 2cm from cast-on edge, ending with RS facing for next row.

Change to 3.25mm needles and work 12 (14: 14: 16: 16: 18) rows in st st, ending with RS facing for next row.

Cont in st st throughout, dec 1 st at each end of next row and every foll 10th row until 95 (101: 107: 113: 119: 125) sts rem.

Work 9 (11: 11: 11: 13: 13) rows straight, ending with RS facing for next row.

Inc 1 st at each end of next row and every foll 10th (10th: 10th: 12th: 12th: 12th) row until there are 105 (113: 119: 125: 131: 137) sts.

Cont straight until back measures 30.5 (32: 33.5: 35: 34: 36)cm from cast-on edge, ending with RS facing for next row.

Shape armhole

Cast off 4 (4: 4: 5: 6: 7) sts at beg of next 2 rows.

Dec 1 st at each end of next 4 (5: 7: 7: 8: 8) rows and then on foll 5 (6: 6: 7: 7: 8) alt rows. *79 (83: 85: 87: 89: 91) sts.*

Cont straight until armhole measures 19 (20: 21: 22: 23: 24)cm, ending with RS facing for next row.

Shape shoulders and neck

Cast off 8 sts at beg of next 2 rows. *63 (67: 69: 71: 73: 75) sts.*

Next row: Cast off 8 sts, k until there are 10 (11: 12: 12: 12: 13) sts on right-hand needle, then turn, leaving rem sts on a holder.

Work on these 10 (11: 12: 12: 12: 13) sts.

Cast off 4 sts at beg of next row.

Cast off rem 6 (7: 8: 8: 8: 9) sts.

With RS facing, rejoin yarn to rem sts and cast off 27 (29: 29: 31: 33: 33) centre sts, work to end.

Complete to match first side, reversing all shaping.

Left front

Using 3mm needles, cast on 54 (57: 60: 63: 66: 69) sts.

Work 2cm in k1, p1 rib as for back.

Change to 3.25mm needles and work 12 (14: 14: 16: 16: 18) rows in st st **and at the same time** keep last 5 sts of all RS rows and first 5 sts of all WS rows in k1, p1 rib for centre front bands.

Cont in st st throughout, dec 1 st at beg of next row and every foll 10th row until 51 (54: 57: 60: 63: 66) sts rem.

Work 9 (11: 11: 11: 13: 13) rows straight, ending with RS facing for next row.

Inc 1 st at beg of next row and every foll 10th (10th: 10th: 12th: 12th: 12th) row until there are 57 (60: 63: 66: 69: 71) sts.

Cont straight until front matches back to armhole, ending with RS facing for next row.

Shape armhole

Cast off 4 (4: 4: 5: 6: 7) sts at beg of next row. *53 (56: 59: 61: 63: 64) sts.*

Work 1 row.

Dec 1 st at armhole edge of next 4 (5: 7: 7: 8: 8) rows and then on foll 5 (6: 6: 7: 7: 8) alt rows. *44 (45: 46: 47: 48: 48) sts.*

Cont straight until 23 (23: 23: 25: 27: 27) rows less have been worked before start of shoulder shaping on back, ending with RS facing for next row.

Shape neck

Cast off 16 sts, work to end of row.

28 (29: 30: 31: 32: 35) sts.
Dec 1 st at neck edge on next
2 rows, then on foll 2 (2: 2: 3: 4: 4)
alt rows, then on every foll 4th row
until 22 (23: 24: 24: 24: 25) sts rem.
Work 9 (9: 9: 9: 9: 13) rows straight,
ending at armhole edge.
Shape shoulder
Cast off 8 sts at beg of next and
foll alt row.
Work 1 row.
Cast off rem 6 (7: 8: 8: 8: 9) sts.

Right front
Work as for left front, but reverse all
shaping.

Sleeves (make 2)
Using 3mm needles, cast on
55 (57: 59: 61: 63: 63) sts.
Work 7cm in k1, p1 rib as for back,
inc at each end of every 7th row.
Change to 3.25mm needles.
Working in st st throughout, cont to
inc 1 st at each end of every 7th
row until there are 81 (83: 85: 87:
89: 91) sts.
Cont straight until sleeve measures
30.5 (32: 33: 34: 35.5: 37)cm from
cast-on edge, ending with RS facing
for next row.
Shape top

Cast off 4 (4: 4: 5: 5: 5) sts at beg
of next 2 rows.
73 (75: 77: 77: 79: 81) sts.
Dec 1 st at each end of next 4 (5: 7:
7: 7: 7) rows.
Work 1 row.
Dec 1 st at each end of next row
and every foll 2 (2: 3: 3: 4: 4) alt
rows, then on foll alt row until 39
(41: 41: 41: 41: 43) sts rem.
Cast off 4 sts at beg of next 2 rows.
Cast off rem sts.

To embroider
Weave in any loose yarn ends.
Enlarge floral motifs to desired size
on a photocopier (approximately
200 %). Use these as templates for
embroidery.
Embroider stems in stem stitch,
using metallic yarn or embroidery
thread. Sew on sequins and beads
where indicated.

To prepare lining
If you wish to line cardigan, lay
lining fabric out flat and trace
outline of each front and back onto
fabric, adding 3cm all around for
seam allowance. Cut out each piece,
then sew lining together at shoulders
and side seams and set aside.

Neck edging
Sew shoulder seams.
With RS facing and using 3mm
needles, pick up and k 37 (37: 37:
38: 39: 39) sts along right front
neck, 35 (37: 37: 39: 41: 41) sts
across back neck, and 37 (37: 37:
38: 39: 39) sts along left front neck.
109 (111: 111: 115: 119: 119) sts.
K 1 row.
Cast off knitwise.

To finish
Set in sleeves and sew sleeve and
side seams.
If lining is desired, insert lining
and sew in place, inside selvedge
edge along neck, insde ribbing
along front bands and along
armhole seam.
Sew buttons to right front band,
positioning them an equal distance
apart. Sew on press studs
underneath button positions.

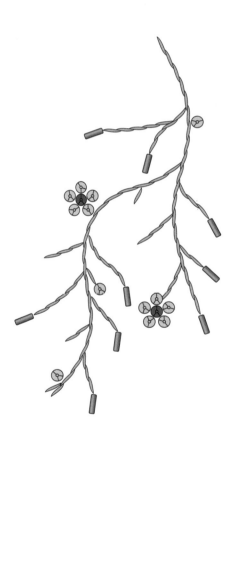

pale pink sequin
pale green sequin
bronze sequin
gold bugle bead
bronze stem stitch

embroidered
clutch bag

materials

Any fine-weight 4ply cotton yarn, such as Yeoman's *Cotton Cannele*
 A: 1 x 250g cone or 340m in ecru
 B: 1 x 250g cone or 340m in string
Pair of 4mm knitting needles
Approximately 50cm of lining fabric and matching sewing thread
Approximately 3m of satin ribbon, 2.5cm wide
Gold embroidering ribbon
Lilac, green and turquoise embroidery thread
Pink beads or sequins

size

One size, approximately 25cm long by 15.5cm wide

tension

30 sts and 48 rows to 10cm over st patt using 4mm needles
 and yarn double

embroidered clutch bag

pattern note

• Use one strand of A together with one strand of B throughout.

To make bag

Using 4mm needles and one strand of yarn A and one strand of B tog, cast on 75 sts.

Row 1 (RS): K1, *bring yarn to front of work between needles – called *yarn front* –, sl 1 purlwise, take yarn to back of work between two needles – called *yarn back* –, k1, rep from * to end.

Row 2: P2, *yarn back, sl 1 purlwise, yarn front, p1, rep from * to last st, p1.

Rep last 2 rows until bag measures 44cm from cast-on edge.

Cast off.

To embroider

Weave in any loose yarn ends. Press pieces gently using a warm iron over a damp cloth.

Use floral motif on opposite page as a guide for embroidery (it is shown actual size).

Embroider outlines and fill in areas as indicated in diagram, adding beads or sequins as desired.

To line

Cut a piece of lining fabric to same size as bag, adding 1.5cm all around for seam allowance. Turn under 1.5cm all around and press.

Hand sew lining neatly in place to WS of bag.

To finish

Fold in 14cm to WS of bag at one end to make pocket, leaving 16cm to create flap.

Fold ribbon in half lengthways and press.

Starting at one corner of pocket, sandwich both layers of bag between ribbon and pin. Sew ribbon in place, making sure that it is even on both sides. Sew ribbon all around edge of bag, mitring corners for a neat finish.

- pink glass bead
- backstitch in gold ribbon
- lilac satin stitch
- green satin stitch
- turquoise stem stitch

yarns

Although I have recommended a specific yarn for many of the projects in the book, you can substitute others. A description of each of the yarns used is given below.

If you decide to use an alternative yarn, choose a yarn that is of the same weight and type. Purchase a substitute yarn that is as close as possible to the original in thickness, weight and texture so that it will work with the pattern instructions. Buy only one ball to start with, so you can test the effect. Calculate the number of balls you will need by meterage rather than by weight. The recommended knitting-needle size and knitting tension on the ball bands are extra guides to the yarn thickness.

To obtain Colinette, Debbie Bliss, Rowan or Yeoman yarns, look up the websites given below to find a mail-order stockist or store in your area:

www.colinette.co.uk
www.knitrowan.com
www.debbieblissonline.com
www.yeoman-yarns.co.uk

Colinette *Giotto*

A chunky-weight ribbon/tape yarn
Recommended knitting-needle size: 8mm
Tension: 11 sts x 16 rows per 10cm over knitted st st
Hank size: 144m per 100g hank
Yarn specification: 50% cotton, 40% rayon, 10% nylon

Debbie Bliss *Maya*

A chunky-weight wool yarn
Recommended knitting-needle size: 5.5mm
Tension: 16 sts x 22 rows per 10cm over knitted st st
Ball size: 126m per 100g ball
Yarn specification: 100% wool

Jaeger *Silk 4ply*

A 4ply-weight silk yarn
Recommended knitting-needle size: 3mm
Tension: 28 sts x 38 rows per 10cm over knitted st st
Ball size: 186m per 50g ball
Yarn specification: 100% silk

Louisa Harding *Fauve Tape*

A chunky-weight synthetic ribbon/tape yarn
Recommended knitting-needle size: 7mm
Tension: 20 sts x 28 rows per 10cm over knitted st st
Ball size: 116m per 50g ball
Yarn specification: 100% nylon

Louisa Harding *Sari Ribbon*

A chunky-weight synthetic ribbon/tape yarn
Recommended knitting-needle size: 8mm
Tension: 12 sts x 16 rows per 10cm over knitted st st
Ball size: 60m per 50g ball
Yarn specification: 90% polyamide, 10% metallic fibre

Rowan *Big Wool*

A super-chunky-weight wool yarn
Recommended knitting-needle size: 15mm
Tension: 7.5 sts x 10 rows per 10cm over knitted st st
Ball size: 80m per 100g ball
Yarn specification: 100% merino wool

Rowan *Kidsilk Haze*

A fine-weight mohair blend yarn
Recommended knitting-needle size: 3.25–5mm
Tension: 18–25 sts x 23–24 rows per 10cm over knitted st st
Ball size: 210m per 25g ball
Yarn specification: 70% super kid mohair, 30% silk

Rowan *Kidsilk Night*

A fine-weight mohair blend yarn
Recommended knitting-needle size: 3.25–5mm
Tension: 18–25 sts x 23–24 rows per 10cm over knitted st st
Ball size: 208m per 25g ball
Yarn specification: 67% super kid mohair, 18% silk, 10% polyester, 5% nylon

Rowan *Lurex Shimmer*

A fine-weight metallic yarn
Recommended knitting-needle size: 3.25mm
Tension: 29 sts x 41 rows per 10cm over knitted st st
Ball size: 95m per 25g ball
Yarn specification: 80% viscose, 20% polyester

Rowan RYC *Cashcotton 4ply*

A 4ply-weight cotton-blend yarn

Recommended knitting-needle size: 4mm

Tension: 22 sts x 30 rows per 10cm over knitted st st

Ball size: 180m per 50g ball

Yarn specification: 35% cotton, 25% polyamide, 18% angora, 18% viscose, 9% cashmere

Rowan *RYC Cashsoft DK*

An double-knitting weight wool-blend yarn

Recommended knitting-needle size: 4mm

Tension: 22 sts x 30 rows per 10cm over knitted st st

Ball size: 130m per 50g ball

Yarn specification: 57% merino wool, 33% microfibre, 10% cashmere

Rowan *RYC Soft Lux*

A medium-weight wool blend yarn

Recommended knitting-needle size: 4.5mm

Tension: 19 sts x 25 rows per 10cm over knitted st st

Ball size: 125m per 50g ball

Yarn specification: 64% merino wool, 10% angora, 24% nylon, 2% metallic fibre

Rowan *Soft Baby*

A medium-weight wool-blend yarn

Recommended knitting-needle size: 4.5mm

Tension: 20 sts x 28 rows per 10cm over knitted st st

Ball size: 150m per 50g ball

Yarn specification: 50% wool, 30% polyamide, 20% cotton

Yeoman *Cotton Cannele 4ply*

A fine-weight 4ply mercerized cotton yarn

Recommended knitting-needle size: 2.75mm

Tension: 33 sts x 44 rows per 10cm over knitted st st

Cone size: 850m per 250g cone

Yarn specification: 100% cotton

abbreviations

alt	alternate
beg	begin(ning)
cm	centimetre(s)
cn	cable needle
cont	continu(e)(ing)
dec	decreas(e)(ing)
garter st	garter stitch (k every row)
foll	follow(s)(ing)
g	gramme(s)
inc	increas(e)(ing)
k	knit
m	metre(s)
m1	make one stitch by picking up horizontal loop before next stitch and knitting into the back of it
mm	millimetre(s)
p	purl
patt	pattern
psso	pass slipped stitch over
rem	remain(ing)
rep	repeat
rev st st	reverse stocking stitch (p all RS rows, k all WS rows)
RS	right side
skp	slip 1, k1, psso
sk2p	slip 1, k2tog, psso
sl	slip
st(s)	stitch(es)
st st	stocking stitch (k all RS rows, p all WS rows)
tog	together
WS	wrong side
tbl	through back of loop(s)
yfwd	yarn forward
yon	yarn over needle

acknowledgements

My personal thanks and appreciation go to the exceptional people who have collaborated to create this book.

The team at Quadrille Publishing, especially Editorial Director, Jane O'Shea, my mentor, for her constant encouragement and style. Creative Director, Helen Lewis, for her tireless innovation on each new project. Lisa Pendreigh, my wonderful project manager for her rigorous support and inimitable professionalism.

It has been a privilege to have Katya de Grunwald photograph this book; her exceptional and distinctive work, together with stylist Beth Dadswell's unique and inspirational concepts have surpassed my wildest expectations. Thank you also to Anita Keeling our fabulous make-up artist and the beautiful Laure Brosson at Select Model Management.

My heartfelt thanks to Sally Lee, my brilliant project maker, for her constant support, enthusiasm, expertise and friendship. And of course Eva Yates and Sally Harding for their inestimable and meticulous hard work in pattern checking.

Stephen Sheard of Coats Craft UK for consistently championing me and Kate Buller, brand manager of Rowan Yarns and the team for their generosity and enthusiastic support. Also Tony Brooks of Yeoman Yarns for his invaluable assistance.

Finally, this book is dedicated to 'creatives' everywhere who continually excite with their passion for the hand made and who push the boundaries of craft by their enthusiasm and innovation. You are my constant source of inspiration.